Grammar Practice 1

L. MARIANI

Longman

his - ОМ
her - ома

Look!
CAPITAL LETTERS
Hello! **I**'m **J**ohn.
Good morning, **M**rs **H**ope.
That's **P**rince **C**harles.

1 Write the sentences. Use capital letters where necessary.

my names' paul. what's your name?

My name's Paul. . . . .

What's your name? . . . .

1. who's that? that's princess diana.

Who fust ?
That's _ _ _ _ _ . . . .

2. this is mr green. he's andy's teacher.

. . . .

. . . .

3. her name's sue. she's kate's friend.

. . . .

. . . .

4. good evening, miss harris. how are you?

. . . .

. . . .

5. i'm fine, thanks.

. . . . *How are you?* . . . . . .
I'm fine, thanks!

6. the name of my school is castle hill school.

. . . .

. . . .

2 Write the questions.

What's your name? . . . .
My name's Andy.

What's her name? . . . .
Her name's Lucy.

1. . . . . *your* . . . .
My name's Kate.

2. . . . . *her* . . . .
Her name's Sue.

3. . . . . *his* . . . .
His name's John.

4. . . . . *her* . . . .
Her name's Cleo.

5. . . . . *your* . . . .
My name's Charles.

6. . . . . *his* . . . .
His name's Ben.

3 Write the answers.

What's your name? (Paul)
My name's Paul. . . . .

What's her name? (Liz)
Her name's Liz. . . . .

1. What's her name? (Sophia)
Her name's sophia . . . .

2. What's his name? (Robert)
His name's Robert . . . .

3. What's your name? (. . . . .)
My name's Yustyna . . . .

4. What's his name? (Peter)
His name's Peter . . . .

5. What's her name? (Sylvia)
Her name's sylvia . . . .

Look!

8:30   **Good morning**, Mr Morgan.

14:30   **Good afternoon**, Mrs Morgan.

19:30   **Good evening**, Miss Harris.

1. 9:30 (Mrs Forbes) — *pau*
   ...Good morning...

2. 15:15 (Mr Clifford)
   ...Good afternoon...

3. 19:45 (Miss Harrap)
   ...Good evening...

4. 13:45 (Mrs Penn)
   ...Good afternoon...

4 **Greet the people.**

7:15 (Miss Gibbon)

Good morning, Miss Gibbon......

20:15 (Mr Parker)

Good evening, Mr Parker.......

5. 10:30 (Mr Hunter)
   ...god morning...

6. 20:00 (Miss Mason)
   ...good evening...

Look!
Andy and Kate are twins.
Andy – **He**'s Kate's brother.
Kate – **She**'s Andy's sister.

5 **Look at this family tree. Write a sentence for each name.**

Mr Morgan ——————— Mrs Morgan

Kate   Lucy   Andy

(Andy) He's Kate's......... brother.

1. (Lucy) She is Kate's sister

2. (Mr Morgan) He's Kate's father

3. (Mrs Morgan) She's Kate's mother

(Kate) She's Lucy's sister.

4. (Mr Morgan) He's Lucy's father

5. (Andy) He is Lucy's brother

6. (Mrs Morgan) He's Lucy's mother

(Mrs Morgan) She's Andy's mother

7. (Mr Morgan) He's Andy's father

8. (Kate) She's Andy sister

9. (Lucy) She's Andy's sister

Look!

Long	Short	
I am	I'm	Kate.
You are	You're	my friend.
He is	He's	my brother.
She is	She's	my sister.
His name is	His name's	John.
Her name is	Her name's	Cleo.

We are	We're	twins.
They are	They're	friends.
What is	What's	your name?
Who is	Who's	that?
That is	That's	my teacher.
This is	------	my cat.

6 Write the sentences, using the short verb forms.

He is my father.

<u>He's my father.</u>

1. What is her name?

   <u>What's her name?</u>

2. She is my teacher.

   <u>She's my father.</u>

3. Who is that?

   <u>Who's that</u>

4. That is Andy.

   <u>That's Andy</u>

5. We are twins.

   <u>We're twins</u>

6. My name is George.

   <u>My name's George</u>

7. I am your friend.

   <u>I'm your friend</u>

Look!

GENITIVE APOSTROPHE 's
He's (He is) Andy**'s** teacher.
She's (She is) Kate**'s** friend.

7 Write the sentences, using the long verb forms.

I'm Kate's mother.

<u>I am Kate's mother.</u>

1. His name's Mr Morgan.

   <u>His name is Mr. Morgan</u>

2. He's Andy's father.

   <u>He is Andy's father</u>

3. What's your friend's name?

   <u>What is your friend's name?</u>

4. Her name's Sue.

   <u>Her name is Sue</u>

5. Who's that?

   <u>Who is that</u>

6. That's Kate's teacher.

   <u>That is Kate's teacher</u>

8 Write the answers in the correct places.

Hello, Mrs Morgan.   Her name's Sheila.
That's my teacher.   Goodbye, Mr Parker.
My name's Liz.   I'm fine, thanks.

What's your name?

<u>My name's Liz</u>

1. How are you?

   <u>I'm fine, thanks</u>

2. Who's that?

   <u>That's my teacher</u>

3. Hello, John.

   <u>Hello, Mrs. Morgan.</u>

4. What's her name?

   <u>Her name's Sheila</u>

5. Bye, Mark.

   <u>Goodbay, Mr. Parker.</u>

Look!

Subject	I	you	he	she	we	they
Adjective	my	your	his	her	our	their

9 | Write the missing words.

Hello! ... _I_ ... 'm Kate. And this is ... _my_ ... brother. ... _his_ ... name's Andy.

1. That's Miss Harris. ... _she_ ...'s Kate's teacher.
2. This is Peter. ... _He_ ...'s a friend from school.
3. Good morning, Mr Morgan. ... _y_ ... 'm Andy's teacher.
4. That's Kate's mother. ... _Her_ ... name's Mrs Morgan.
5. Hello! ... _My_ ... name's Jack.
6. How are ... _you_ ...?
7. JOHN: Who's that?

   ANDY: That's Kate. ... _We_ ... 're twins.
8. That's Andy's father. ... _His_ ... name's Mr Morgan.

Grammar check

Write the missing words.

	..._your_...	name?
What's	..._her_...	
	..._his_...	

		Kate.
..._My_...	name's	Sue.
..._his_...		Andy.
..._Her_...		

I ..._'m_... Paul.	
You ..._'re_...	
He ..._is_...	a friend from school.
She ..._is_...	
We ..._'re_... twins.	

		Mr	
Good	..._morning,_..		
	..._afternoon_	_Mrs_	Smith.
	..._evening_	_M.S._	
Goodbye,			

one	_six_
too	_seven_
three	_eight_
four	_nine_
five	_ten_

5

Look!				
CAPITAL LETTERS				
Names:			Andy, Kate, Mr Morgan,	
			Castle Hill School	
Roads:			49, Foster Street;	
			75, King's Road	
Cities/towns:			London, Dover	
Countries:			China, India, England	
Nationalities:			Chinese, Indian, English	
Start of sentence:			His name's Martin.	
			He's a student.	
… and *I*!			Kate and **I** are twins.	

1 | Write this passage. Use capital letters where necessary.

my name's paul roberts. i'm twenty years old. i'm american, but i live in england now. my address is 88, carlton street, london, and my telephone number is 01 559 7401. i'm a student at queen's college. my teachers are miss grey and mr hogwood. i have an english friend called mary.

My name's Paul Roberts ....

....

....

....

....

....

....

....

3 | Write the numbers in sentences.

What's your telephone number? (754 8362) It's seven-five-four-eight-three-six-two.

1. What's her favourite number? (14) *fourteen* It is nine-six-one-four five, seven, eight

2. What's his telephone number? (961 4578) ....

3. What's your address? (42, Station Road) .... forty-two

4. What's his favourite number? (25) .... twenty-five

5. What's her address? (54, Park Road) ....

6. What's your favourite number? (33) ....

Look!		you?	I'm	
	are			
How old		they	We They	're	eleven (years old).
	is	he? she?	He She	's	

2 | Write questions and answers.

John? (15)

How old is John?

He's fifteen.

they? (20)

How old are they?

They're twenty.

1. you? (13)

How old are you? old

I'm thirteen years old

2. Miss Robson? (24)

How old is Miss Robson?

She's twenty-four

3. he? (30)

How old is he?

He's thirty

4. Mr Parker? (43)

How old is Mr. Parker?

He's forty-three

5. Mark and Sheila? (14)

How old are Mark and Sheila?

They're fourteen

Look!

What's **this**?
It's a comic.

What's **that**?
It's a book.

4 Write questions and answers.

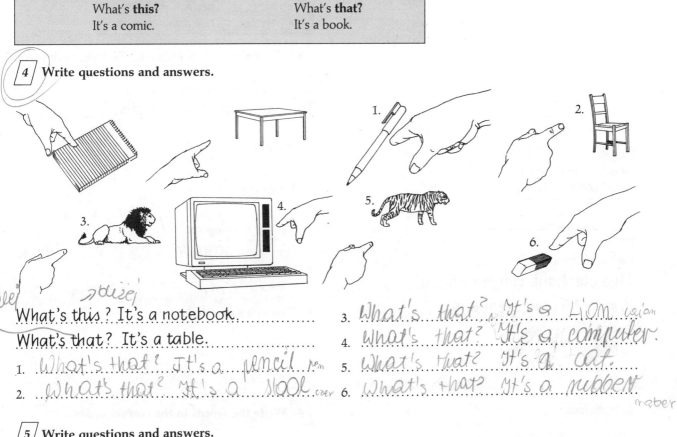

What's this? It's a notebook.

What's that? It's a table.

1. What's that? It's a pencil. ᵖᵉⁿ

2. What's that? It's a stool. ᵗˢᵗᵒᵒˡ

3. What's that? It's a lion. ˡᵃⁱᵒⁿ

4. What's that? It's a computer.

5. What's that? It's a cat.

6. What's that? It's a rubber. ʳᵘᵇᵉʳ

5 Write questions and answers.

(pencil?)   Is it a pencil? Yes, it is.

(desk?)   Is it a desk? No, it isn't. It's a table.

1. (computer?) ....

....

2. (lion?) ....

....

3. (notebook?) ....

....

4. (lion?) ....

....

5. (panda?) ....

....

6 Write the words in the correct columns.

America African Chinese India English
China Africa Indian England American

Countries   *Nationalities*
America   American

1. Africa   African
2. China   Chinese
3. India   Indian
4. England   English

Look!

| a lion | an elephant |
| a tiger | an Indian tiger |

7 Describe the animals.

elephant/Africa
This elephant is from Africa.
It's an African elephant.

1. panda/China
This panda is from China.
It's an Chinese panda.

2. tiger/India
This tiger is from India.
It's an Indian tiger.

3. bald eagle/America
This bald eagle is from America.
It's an American bald eagle.

4. lion/Africa
This lion is from Africa.
It's an African lion.

5. sheep dog/England
This sheep dog is from England.
It's an English sheep dog.

Look!

Long	Short	
I am	I'm	Paul.
I am not	I'm not	a student.
It is	It's	a rubber.
It is not	It isn't	a ruler.
They are	They're	twins.
They are not	They aren't	friends.

8 Write the sentences, using the long verb forms.

It's an English sheep dog.
It is an English sheep dog.

1. I'm twelve and a half.
I am twelve and a half

2. They're fourteen.
They are fourteen

3. It's Andy's computer.
It is Andy is computer

4. I'm not thirteen.
I am not thirteen

5. That isn't Kate's desk.
That isn

6. It's Mr Green's book.
It is Mr Green is book

9 Write the words in the correct order.

an / It's / elephant / African
It's an African elephant.

1. it / Where / from? / is
Where

2. number / 49675 / telephone / His / is
His is number telephone

3. panda / from / is / China / This
This is panda from China

4. your / What's / number? / telephone
What's your telephone numb

5. is / old / tiger / years / thirteen / That
That

10 Write the questions in the correct places.

What's this?   *How old are you?*   *Where is it from?*
Is it a comic?   *What's her address?*   *Are you twelve?*
What's his telephone number?

What's her address? ....
It's 81, Cardiff Road.

1. ....
    No, it isn't. It's a notebook.

2. *Who is it?* ....
    It's a tiger.

3. *How old are you?* ....
    I'm twelve.

4. *What's your telep. mom.?* ....
    It's 788 3598.

5. *You are ?dish?* ....
    Yes, I am.

6. *Where are you from?* ....
    It's from England.

Grammar check

Write the missing words.

How old	are	you?
		they?
	is	..........?
		..........?
		..........?

I......	....	
We...	....	
....	....	twelve (years old).
He....		
....	....	
....		

Are you eleven?	Yes, I '.m...
	No, I'm.... not... I'm twelve.
Is it a pencil?	Yes, it is....
	No, ... not. It's a pen.

This	is	.... panda.
That		.... eagle.

Where is it ....?	It's from China.

12 twelve	20 twenty
13 thirteen	30 thirty
... .	... .
... .	... .
... .	... .
... .	... .
... .	... .
... .	... .
100 a hundred	

Test your English

1 Circle the correct answer.

RICK: Hello! I'm Rick.			
ANNA: Hi! .... name's Anna.	a) I	(b) My	c) Your
RICK: How old are you, Anna?			
ANNA: I (1) .... thirteen.	a) 's	b) are	c) 'm
And that's (2) .... brother.	a) my	b) your	c) his
RICK: What's (3) .... name?	a) her	b) he's	c) his
ANNA: Thomas. But he's called Tom.			
(4) .... 're twins.	a) They	b) You	c) We

MIKE: (5) .... 's that, Jane?	a) What	b) Who	c) Where
JANE: That's my sister. (6) .... name's Pat.	a) His	b) Her	c) My
MIKE: How old is (7) ....?	a) she	b) her	c) he
JANE: Eleven and a half. And that's			
(8) .... little brother, Bob.	a) your	b) his	c) our

MRS PENN: (9) .... you twelve, Rita?	a) Is	b) Are	c) Am
RITA: No, I'm not. I'm thirteen.			
MRS PENN: (10) .... 's your address?	a) Where	b) Who	c) What
RITA: (11) .... 5, Station Road.	a) It	b) It's	c) Its
MRS PENN: Thank you, Rita. (12)	a) Goodbye!	b) Hello!	c) Good morning!

ANDY: (13) .... 's this, Mr Green?	a) Who	b) How	c) What
MR GREEN: It's (14) .... eagle.	a) one	b) an	c) a
ANDY: Is it from Africa?			
MR GREEN: No, it (15)	a) is	b) isn't	c) 's
It's from North America.			

Total. ..... /15

2 Write the words in the correct places.

> I He She my His Her am is a of 's

Hello! My name is Julie Cross. ....I.... am twelve years old. My address is
73, Portland Road, Newcastle, and (1) ...My... telephone number
(2) ...is a... 472 9953.

I have (3) ...a.... brother. (4) ...His... name's David. (5) ...He...
is fourteen.

I (6) ...am.... a student. The name (7) ....is... my school is New
Street School. My teacher (8) ...s..... name is Miss Bartlett. (9) ...she...
is a very good teacher.

I have a friend at school. (10) ...her... name is Maria.

Total. ..... /10

3 Write the correct answers from the list on the right.

GEORGE: Hello. I'm George. What's your name?

PAULA: (E) My name's Paula.

GEORGE: Are you English?

PAULA: (1) Yes, I'm

GEORGE: How old are you?

PAULA: (2) I'm twelve and a half

Who's that?

GEORGE: (3) It's a computer

PAULA: What's his name?

GEORGE: (4) (J)

PAULA: How old is he?

GEORGE: (5) He's ten

PAULA: Look, this is my new address book. What's your address?

GEORGE: (6) It's Dover 24578 C

PAULA: And your telephone number?

GEORGE: (7) It's Dover 24578

Look at this.

PAULA: Is it a calculator?

GEORGE: (8) No, It isn't

PAULA: What is it?

GEORGE: (9) That's my brother

PAULA: Mm, it's great. Well, I must go now. Bye!

GEORGE: (10) Bye, Paula

A. That's my brother.
B. It's a computer.
C. It's 9, Park Road.
D. Yes, I am.
E. My name's Paula.
F. It's Dover 24578.
G. Bye, Paula.
H. I'm twelve and a half.
I. No, it isn't.
J. Richard. But he's called Rick.
K. He's ten.

Total. . . . . /10

Grand Total. . . . . /35

1 Match the pairs. Then write the words in the correct columns.

		Countries	Nationalities
Brazil	Spain	Brazil	Brazilian
German	Japanese	Germany	German
1. Italy	Greek	1. Italy	Italian
2. Turkish	Turkey	2. Turkish	Turkey
3. Japan	Argentinian	3. Japan	Japanese
4. The USA	France	4. USA	American
5. Greece	Brazilian	5. Greece	Greek
6. Spanish	American	6. Spain	Spanish
7. Argentina	Germany	7. Argentina	Argentinian
8. French	British	8. France	French
9. Britain	Italian	9. British	Britain

2 Write the answers.

Where's Yukiko from? (Japan)

She's from Japan. She's Japanese.

Where's John from? (Britain)

He's from Britain. He's British.

1. Where's Pamela from? (Spain)

   ....

2. Where's Mr Brown from? (The USA)

   ....

3. Where's Mrs Hernandez from? (Argentina)

   ....

4. Where's Isabelle from? (France)

   ....

5. Where's Mr Theodorakis from? (Greece)

   ....

6. Where's Carlos from? (Brazil)

   ....

7. Where's Maria from? (Turkey)

   ....

8. Where are you from? (Italy)

   ....

Look!				I am.			I'm not.	
Are you		Spanish?	Yes,	he/she is.		No,	he/she isn't.	
Is	he she			we	are.		we	aren't.
Are they				they			they	

3 **Write questions.**

Maria/Turkish?

Is Maria Turkish ? ....

Kate and Andy/English?

Are Kate and Andy English ? ....

1. Sylvia/Greek?

Ys Sylvia Greek ? ....

2. Paul/American?

Ys Paul american ? ....

3. Carlo and Laura/Italian?

Are Carlo and Laura Italian?

4. Mr Reuter/German?

Ys Mr. Reuter German?

5. Mrs Domingo/Brazilian?

Ys Mrs. Domingo Brazilian?

6. Mr and Mrs Toyota/Japanese?

Are Mr. and Mrs Taylor Japanese?

7. you/English?

Are you Ynglish ?

4 **Write answers using** Yes, (✓) **or** No (✗).

Are you Italian?

✓ Yes, I am ....

Is Mrs Smith American?

✗ No, she isn't ....

1. Are you German?

✗ No I'm not

2. Is Mr Valdez Brazilian?

✓ Yes he is

3. Are they from Japan?

✓ Yes they are

4. Is Anna Spanish?

✗ No she isn't

5. Are Charles and Paul French?

✗ No they are not

6. Are you a student?

✓ Yes I'm

7. Is Miss Thompson American?

✓ Yes she is

8. Is Roberto from Argentina?

✗ No he is not

1. .... ✗

2. .... ✓

Look!

Long	Short	
I am not	I'm not	English.
You are not	You aren't	Spanish.
He is not	He isn't	a student.
She is not	She isn't	from the USA.
We are not	We aren't	Brazilian.
They are not	They aren't	from France.
Where is	Where's	she from?

5 **Write the sentences, using the long verb forms.**

She isn't Kate's friend.

She is not Kate's friend.

1. Peter isn't American.

   Peter is not American

2. Mr and Mrs Pellier aren't French.

   Mr and Mrs Pellier are not

3. She isn't Pat's teacher.

   She is not Pat's teacher

4. Miguel isn't from Argentina.

   Miguel is not from Argentina

5. Where's he from?

   Where is he from?

6. I'm not Anne's brother.

   I am not Anne's brother

7. Mary's eyes aren't blue.

   Mary's eyes are not blue

Look!

COUNTABLE		UNCOUNTABLE
Singular	Plural	
a sweet	**some** sweets	**some** chewing gum
an orange	**some** oranges	**some** liquorice

6 **Offer and accept (✓) or refuse (✗).**

Do you want a chocolate?
☑ Yes, please

Do you want some liquorice?
☒ No, thanks

1. Do you want a banana?
   ☒ No, thanks

2. Do you want gum?
   ☑ Yes, please

3. Do you want a
   ☒ No, thanks

4. Do you want a (lolly)
   ☑ Yes, please

5. Do you want
   ☑ Yes, please

6. ☒ No, thanks

7 **Write questions and answers.**

(Mary's hair?/black)

What colour is Mary's hair?

It's black.

(your eyes?/blue)

What colour are your eyes?

They're blue.

1. (Linda's eyes?/green)

....

2. (John's hair?/dark brown)

....

....

3. (a tomato?/red)

....

....

4. (George's eyes?/grey)

....

....

5. (your hair?/blonde)

....

....

6. (the sky?/blue)

....

....

7. (Anne's hair?/light brown)

....

....

8 **Write the questions in the correct places.**

Is Maria Spanish? Who's that man?
What colour is your hair? What nationality is he?
Do you want a chocolate? Where's she from?
Are Mr and Mrs West from England?
What are your favourite colours?

What colour is your hair ?

It's brown.

1.

.... He's French.

2.

.... No, they aren't.

3.

.... That's Harrison Ford.

4.

.... Yes, please.

5.

.... She's from Japan.

6.

.... Yes, she is.

7.

.... They're red and blue.

Grammar check

Write the missing words.

Verb to be

Interrogative					*Short answers*										*Positive (short form)*	
Am I						I	..*am*...			I	'm not.		I	...'m...		
Are you						you	*are*.			you	*are not*		You	.*are*.		
Is he						he	i.s....			he	is not		He	is....		
Is she	French?				Yes,	she	.i.s....		No,	she	is not		She	..is....	English.
Is it						it	..i.s....			it	is not		It	..is....		
Are we						we	*are*.			we	*are not*		We	*are*.		
Are you						you	.*are*.			you	*are not*		You	*are*.		
Are they						they	.*are*.			they	*are not*		They	.*are*		

1 **Write questions and answers.**

Jane Robert 1. Mike 2. Kate

3. Mr Robson 4. Lucy 5. Linda 6. Miss Mason

Whose skirt is this ?............................. 3. ....
It's Jane's... ....
Whose socks are these ?...................... 4. ....
They're Robert's.................................. ....

1. .... 5. ....
....
2. .... 6. ....
....

Look!

POSSESSIVES

Adjectives	my	you	his	her	our	their
Pronouns	mine	yours	his	hers	ours	theirs

---

2 **Write answers using** Yes (✓) **or** No (✗).

Is this Maria's blouse?
✓ Yes, it's hers.
Are these Peter's shoes?
✗ No, they aren't his.

1. Is this Mr Porter's coat?
✗ No, it is not his
2. Are these Julia's stamps?
✓ Yes, they are hers
3. Is this your stamp album?
✓ No, it is not mine

4. Is this Anna's dress?
✗ No, it is not her
5. Are these Francisco's jeans?
✗ No, they aren't jeans
6. Are these your stickers?
✓ Yes, they are mine (my)
7. Is this Mrs Stafford's house?
✓ Yes it is his
8. Are these Paul's badges?
✗ No, aren't his

17

Look!

PRONOUNS

Subject	Object
I	me
you	you
he	him
she	her
it	it
we	us
they	them

3 **Answer with** like **or** don't like**.**

I like David Bowie. (great)

Yes, I like him too. I think he's great

I like Sophia. (boring)

I don't like her. I think she's boring

1. I like John. (horrible)

Yes I like him too. I think he's horrible

2. I like Duran Duran. (good)

Yes I like them too. I think them good

3. I like this record. (bad)

No I don't like it. I think is bad

4. I like Tina Turner. (boring)

Not I don't like her I think she's boring

5. I like these posters. (horrible)

No I don't like him I think he's horrible

6. I like Bruce Springsteen. (great)

Yes I like him too. I think he's great

7. I like this book. (fantastic)

Yes I like it too. I think its fantastic

Look!

Have you					I have.			I haven't.	
Has	he she	got	a camera? any badges?	Yes,		he she	has.	No,	he she	hasn't.

4 **Write the questions, using** have **or** has**.**

(you/computer?) *Have you got a computer?*

(Sophia/postcards?) *Has Sophia got any postcards?*

1. (Miss Simpson/cat?) ....

2. (David/foreign stamps?) ....

3. (you/rock star photos?) ....

4. (Mr Green/bike?) ....

5. (you/model trains?) ....

6. (Laura/sleeping bag?) ....

18

5 **Write the answers, using** Yes (✓) **or** No (✗).

Have you got a camera?   ✓   Yes, I have.

Has Michael got any stickers?   ✗   No, he hasn't.

1. Have you got any foreign coins?   ✗ ....

2. Has Sylvia got a tent?   ✓ ....

3. Has Mr Smith got a dog?   ✗ ....

4. Have you got any badges?   ✓ ....

5. Has John got a computer?   ✓ ....

6. Has Pamela got any stickers?   ✗ ....

Look!

I've			I haven't		
He She	's	got **some** posters.	He She	hasn't	got **any** posters.

6 **Write what people have (✓) or haven't (✗) got.**

NAME	POSTERS	BADGES	STICKERS	ROCK STAR PHOTOS	STAMPS
Maria	✓		✓		✗
Tom		✓		✗	✗
Peter	✓	✓	✗		
Liz	✓		✗	✓	
George		✗	✓		✗
Lucy	✗		✗	✓	
Mark	✓	✗			✓
I	✓			✗	✗

Maria's got some posters and some stickers, but she hasn't got any stamps.

Tom's got some badges, but he hasn't got any rock star photos or stamps.

1. ....

2. ....

3. ....

4. ....

5. ....

6. ....

Look!

VERB to have got			VERB to be		
Long	Short		Long	Short	
He has	He's	got a dog.	He is	He's	a teacher.
She has	She's	got a radio.	She is	She's	a student.
			It is	It's	a comic.

Remember:
Genitive possessive 's: Kate's mother.

7 **Write the sentences, using the long verb forms.**

Linda's got some postcards.   Linda has got some postcards.

Henry's my friend.   Henry is my friend.

That's Paul's teacher.   That is Paul's teacher.

1. Mr Brown's got a computer. ....

2. What's this? ....

3. It's Andy's calculator. ....

4. She's got David's records. ....

5. He's Kate's father. ....

6. Who's that? ....

7. That's Miss Key's brother. ....

8. Peter's got a bike. ....

8 **Write the questions in the correct places.**

*Have you got a camera?   Whose book is this?   Has Mary got a radio?   Is this your jacket?
How many have you got?   Are these Tom's jeans?   Who's your favourite pop star?*

Has Mary got a radio?
No, she hasn't.

1. ....
   I like Michael Jackson.

2. ....
   Yes, it's mine.

3. ....
   Yes, they're his.

4. ....
   Nearly two hundred.

5. ....
   It's Mike's.

6. ....
   No, I haven't.

Grammar check

Write the missing words.

This is	my your his her our their	anorak.

It's	...mine.... ....ours.... ...theirs..

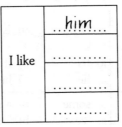

He			pop star.
She	's	my favourite	
It			record.
They're			band.

I like	..him... ....

Verb to have (got): **singular**

Interrogative

....	you	....	a brother?
....	he	....	a sister?
....	she	....	any sisters?

Short answers

Yes,	I	....
	he	....
	she	....

No,	I	....
	he	....
	she	....

Positive (short form)

I	.... a watch.
He	.... a computer.
She	.... some postcards.

Negative (short form)

I	.... a watch.
He	.... a computer.
She	.... any postcards.

Test your English

1 **Circle the correct answer.**

EMMA: Hi! What's your name?			
PAUL: My name's Paul. What's *your*? *name*	a) your	b) you	c) yours (circled)
EMMA: Emma.			
(1) *How* old are you, Paul?	a) What	b) How (circled)	c) Who
PAUL: I'm nearly fifteen.			
EMMA: (2) *Where* are you from?	a) Who	b) Where (circled)	c) How (circled)
PAUL: I'm from England.			
Do you want (3) .... sweet?	a) a	b) some	c) any
EMMA: (4)	a) Thank.	b) No, thanks.	c) No, please.
JOHN: (5) *Whose* poster is this?	a) Whose	b) Who	c) Who's
PETE: It's mine. Look. This is Diego Maradona.			
(6) *He's* from Argentina.	a) He's	b) Is he	c) His
JOHN: Where's that?			
PETE: (7) *It is* in South America, silly!	a) Its	b) It's	c) It
I think Maradona's great. I like (8) *him*.	a) he	b) his	c) him
RITA: Have you got (9) *any* stickers?	a) some	b) any	c) a
JANE: Yes, I (10) *have*	a) 've	b) 've got	c) have
RITA: My (11) .... nearly two hundred stickers.	a) sister's	b) sisters	c) sister's got
I think (12) .... are terrific.	a) their	b) they	c) them
MISS WHITE: Are (13) *these* your trainers, Mary?	a) this	b) that	c) these
MARY: No, they aren't (14) *my*.	a) my	b) mine	c) me
MISS WHITE: Perhaps they're Anna's.			
MARY: Yes, I think they're (15) *hers*	a) her	b) his	c) hers

Total. . . . . /15

2 **Write the words in the correct places.**

She	It	they	him	her	's	are	any	's	from	old

Christina is a new member of the band Crossroads. ..*She*.. is American.

She was born in New York but (1) ..*her*.. parents are (2) .... Mexico.

She is nearly sixteen years (3) ..*old*.. . Her hair is blonde and her eyes

(4) ..*are*.. blue.

Christina (5) ....*'s*... favourite pop star is Paul Young. She likes (6) ..*him*..

very much, but she also likes Duran Duran. She thinks (7) .... are great!

Christina likes collections. She (8) ....*'s*.... got nearly a hundred posters,

but she hasn't got (9) .... stickers or badges. 'I hate badges', she says.

What's her favourite food? (10) ....*It*....'s fish and chips!

Total. . . . . /10

3 Write the correct answers from the list on the right.

MIKE: Hello!

PAT: (F) Hi! ....

MIKE: Are you American?

PAT: (1) Yes, I am ....

MIKE: Where are you from in America?

PAT: (2) From Texas. ....

Do you want a crisp?

MIKE: (3) Yes, I have, please ....

PAT: Here you are.

MIKE: (4) Thanks ....

PAT: What's this?

MIKE: (5) It's my photo album ....

PAT: Hey, is that a picture of Duran Duran?

MIKE: (6) Yes, It is. ....

PAT: Who's your favourite pop star?

MIKE: (7) I like Madona ....

PAT: Yes, I like her too. Have you got any of her records?

MIKE: (8) Yes, I m ....

PAT: How many have you got?

MIKE: (9) ....

PAT: Well, I'm going home now. Goodbye.

MIKE: (10) Bye ....

A.	Yes, please.
B.	About six.
C.	Yes, it is.
D.	From Texas.
E.	Yes, I have.
F.	Hi!
G.	Bye.
H.	Yes, I am.
I.	Thanks.
J.	I like Madonna.
K.	It's my photo album.

Total. . . . . /10

Grand Total. . . . . /35

Look!
The apostrophe
Possession:

This is **Kate's** sweater.
This is **my parents'** bedroom.
This is **Andy and Kate's** house.

Remember:
Verb *to be*   That**'s** Miss Harris. She**'s** my teacher.
Verb *to have (got)*   Andy**'s got** a calculator.

1 Write the sentences, using capital letters and apostrophes where necessary.

thats mr johnsons computer.

That's Mr. Johnson's computer.

1. whats mikes telephone number?

....

2. theres a poster in lucys room.

....

3. wheres mr and mrs morgans house?

....

4. miss greens got two cats.

....

5. its her parents house.

....

6. is this marys jacket?

....

7. yes, its hers.

....

8. his names philip.

....

2 Now rewrite the sentences in exercise 1, using the long verb forms.

That is Mr. Johnson's computer.

1. ....
2. ....
3. ....
4. ....
5. ....
6. ....
7. ....
8. ....

3 Look at the list of Sheila's collections and write questions and answers.

STAMPS	French	75
	Spanish	41
	Turkish	30
COINS	German	13
	Greek	8
	Italian	12
RECORDS	British	68
	American	37

How many French stamps are there?
There are seventy-five.
How many Spanish stamps are there?
There are forty-one.

1. ....
   ....
2. ....
   ....
3. ....
   ....
4. ....
   ....
5. ....
   ....
6. ....
   ....

Look! Is	there	a table	in your room?	Yes, there	is.	No, there	isn't.
Are		any chairs			are.		aren't.

4 Write questions and answers, using Yes (✓) or No (×).

(kitchen?) ✓ Is there a kitchen ? Yes, there is.

(posters?) ✗ Are there any posters ? No, there aren't.

1. (desk?) ✓ ....

2. (bathroom?) ✗ ....

3. (bed?) ✓ ....

4. (cupboards?) ✓ ....

5. (pictures?) ✗ ....

6. (carpet?) ✓ ....

7. (chimney?) ✗ ....

8. (curtains?) ✗ ....

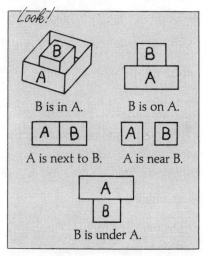

Look!

B is in A.   B is on A.

A is next to B.   A is near B.

B is under A.

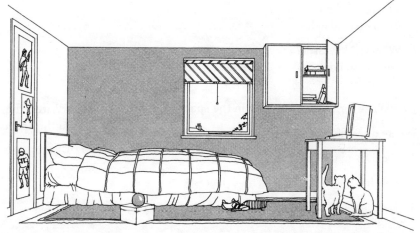

5 Look at the picture, and write questions and answers.

(computer?) Where's the computer ?
It's on the table.

(books?) Where are the books?
They're in the cupboard.

1. (ball?) Where's the ball
It's on the box

2. (trainers?) Where are the traing
They are over the
bed

3. (posters?) Where are the posters
They are on the door

4. (cupboard?) Where's the cupboard
It's on the wall

5. (cats?) where are under the
table

6. (carpet?) Where is the carpet
It's on the floor.

Look!			
(..........) is	in the	north south	of Britain.
	on the	east west	coast of Scotland.

6 Write the answers.

Where's Manchester?
(N/England)

It's in the north of England...

Where's Southampton?
(S/coast/England)

It's on the south coast of England...

1. Where's Cardiff?
(S/coast/Wales)
   ....

2. Where's Norwich?
(E/England)
   ....

3. Where's Aberdeen?
(E/coast/Scotland)
   ....

4. Where's Liverpool?
(NW/coast/England)
   ....

5. Where's Folkestone?
(S/coast/England)
   ....

6. Where's Newcastle?
(NE/coast/England)
   ....

7 Write for, from, of or with in the spaces.

Where do you come ..from...?

1. She lives in the north .... Spain.

2. This town is famous .... its castle.

3. There are five students .... blue eyes in my class.

4. That lion is .... Africa.

5. There are the remains .... a Roman house in Dover.

6. Thank you very much .... the book.

7. There's a table .... three chairs in the kitchen.

8 Write Who, Where, Whose, How or How many in the spaces.

Where.......... 's Dover?

Whose.......... trainers are these?

1. .... 's that man?

2. .... foreign stamps has Anna got?

3. .... do you live?

4. .... book is this?

5. .... 's Mrs Thompson from?

6. .... students are there in your class?

7. .... old is your father?

9 **Now write the questions from exercise 8 in the correct places.**

Whose trainers are those? ....
They're Harry's.

Where's Dover ? ....
It's in the south-east of England.

1. ....
   She's from the USA.

2. ....
   She's got nearly four hundred.

3. ....
   I live in the centre of Rome.

4. ....
   He's forty-four.

5. ....
   It's Mr Green's.

6. ....
   That's Mr Morgan.

7. ....
   There are twenty-nine.

Grammar check

Write the missing words.

....	there	a chair	in your room?
....		any chairs	

Yes,	....
	....

No	....
	....

There	.... a castle	in my town.
	.... some gardens	
	aren't .... parks	

Where's (*name of place*)?

It's	.... the	north	of England.
	.... the	....	coast of Scotland.

Where do you live?

I	.... London.	
He	........the centre .... Liverpool.	
She		

1 Write questions and responses.

wallet   Do you want a wallet or a purse?

purse ✓   Can I have a purse, please?

foreign coins ✓   Do you want some foreign coins or some foreign stamps?

foreign stamps   Can I have some foreign coins, please?

1. comb   ....

    brush ✓   ....

2. radio   ....

    camera ✓   ....

3. jeans ✓   ....

    trainers   ....

4. football   ....

    tennis racket ✓   ....

5. badges ✓   ....

    stickers   ....

Look!

Can	you he she we they	speak English?	Yes,	I he she we they	can.	No,	I he she we they	can't.

2 Write questions and answers, using Yes or No.

(Peter/ride a horse?/Yes)

Can Peter ride a horse?

Yes, he can.

(Sheila/play the guitar?/No)

Can Sheila play the guitar?

No, she can't.

1. (Mrs Morgan/play the piano?/Yes)

....

....

2. (Paul/use a computer?/No)

....

....

3. (you/climb a rope?/Yes)

....

....

4. (Kate and Andy/dive?/Yes)

....

5. (Mr Harrison/speak Spanish?/No)

....

6. (your friends/swim under water?/No)

....

....

3 Write what people can (✓) or cannot (✗) do.

	Anna	George	Paul and Mary	John	Miss Turner	Mr West
speak German	✓					
speak French	✗					
ride a horse						✓
play tennis				✓		✗
dive		✓		✗		
swim under water		✗				
play the guitar					✓	
play the piano					✗	
use a calculator			✓			
use a computer			✗			

Anna can speak German but she can't speak French. ....

1. ....
2. ....
3. ....
4. ....
5. ....

Look!

VERBS + -ing
watch + -ing = *watching*   BUT   write + -ing = *writing*
play + -ing = *playing*   make + -ing = *making*
look + -ing = *looking*   run + -ing = *running*

4 Write the -ing form of the verb.

help   helping...............   4. play ....
use   using...................   5. sit ....
1. write ....   6. spell ....
2. show ....   7. dive ....
3. knit ....   8. drop ....

Look!						
What	are	you they	doing?	I'm		writing a letter.
				He She	's	
	is	he she		We They	're	

5 **Look at the pictures and write the answers.**

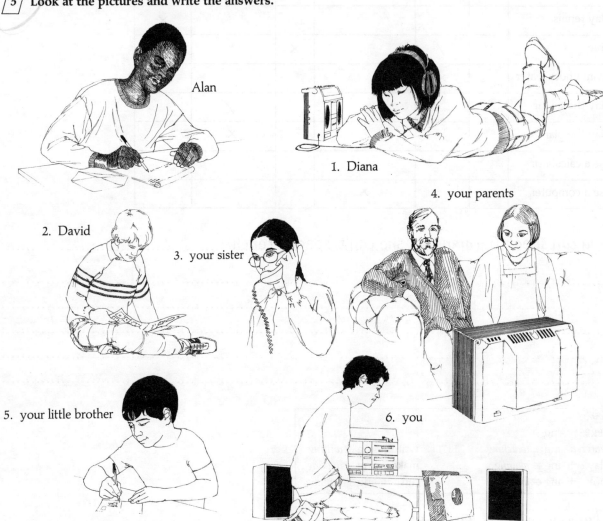

Alan

1. Diana

4. your parents

2. David

3. your sister

5. your little brother

6. you

What is Alan doing?

He's writing a letter. ....

1. What is Diana doing?

   ....

2. Oh. And David? What is he doing?

   ....

3. What about your sister?

   ....

4. And your parents?

   ....

5. I see. What is your little brother doing?

   ....

6. Well, what are you doing?

   ....

Answer key

LESSONS 1–5

Ex. 1
1. Who's That? That's Princess Diana.
2. This is Mr Green. He's Andy's teacher.
3. Her name's Sue. She's Kate's friend.
4. Good evening, Miss Harris. How are you?
5. I'm fine, thanks.
6. The name of my school is Castle Hill School.

Ex. 2
1. What's your name?
2. What's her name?
3. What's his name?
4. What's her name?
5. What's your name?
6. What's his name?

Ex. 3
1. Her name's Sophia.
2. His name's Robert.
3. My name's . . . .
4. His name's Peter.
5. Her name's Sylvia.

Ex. 4
1. Good morning, Mrs Forbes.
2. Good afternoon, Mr Clifford.
3. Good evening, Miss Harrap.
4. Good afternoon, Mrs Penn.
5. Good morning, Mr Hunter.
6. Good evening, Miss Mason.

Ex. 5
1. She's Kate's sister.
2. He's Kate's father.
3. She's Kate's mother.
4. He's Lucy's father.
5. He's Lucy's brother.
6. She's Lucy's mother.
7. He's Andy's father.
8. She's Andy's sister.
9. She's Andy's sister.

Ex. 6
1. What's her name?
2. She's my tea her.
3. Who's that?
4. That's Andy.
5. We're twins.
6. My name's George.
7. I'm your friend.

Ex. 7
1. His name is Mr Morgan.
2. He is Andy's father.
3. What is your friend's name?
4. Her name is Sue.
5. Who is that?
6. That is Kate's teacher.

Ex. 8
1. I'm fine, thanks.
2. That's my teacher.
3. Hello, Mrs Morgan.
4. Her name's Sheila.
5. Goodbye, Mr Parker.

Ex. 9
1. She   2. He   3. I   4. Her   5. My
6. you   7. We   8. His

GRAMMAR CHECK

We're twins, Good *afternoon/evening Mrs/* Andy.
I'm Paul. *He's/She's* a friend from school.
We're twins. Good *afternoon/evening Mrs/ Miss* Smith . . . *two three four five . . . seven eight nine ten*

LESSONS 6–10

Ex. 1
My name's Paul Roberts. I'm twenty years old. I'm American, but I live in England now. My address is 88, Carlton Street, London, and my telephone number is 01 559 7401. I'm a student at Queen's College. My teachers are Miss Grey and Mr Hogwood. I have an English friend called Mary.

Ex. 2
1. How old are you? I'm thirteen.
2. How old is Miss Robson? She's twenty-four.
3. How old is he? He's thirty.
4. How old is Mr Parker? He's forty-three.
5. How old are Mark and Sheila? They're fourteen.

Ex. 3
1. It's fourteen.
2. It's nine-six-one-four-five-seven-eight.
3. It's forty-two, Station Road.
4. It's twenty-five.
5. It's fifty-four, Park Road.
6. It's thirty-three.

Ex. 4
1. What's this? It's a pen.
2. What's that? It's a chair.
3. What's that? It's a lion.
4. What's this? It's a computer.
5. What's that? It's a tiger.
6. What's this? It's a rubber.

Ex. 5
1. Is it a computer? Yes, it is.
2. Is it a lion? Yes, it is.
3. Is it a notebook? No, it isn't. It's a comic.
4. Is it a lion? No, it isn't. It's a tiger.
5. Is it a panda? Yes, it is.

Ex. 6
1. Africa/African   3. India/Indian
2. China/Chinese   4. England/English

Ex. 7
1. This panda is from China. It's a Chinese panda.
2. This tiger is from India. It's an Indian tiger.
3. This bald eagle is from America. It's a American bald eagle.
4. This lion is from Africa. It's an African lion.
5. This sheep dog is from England. It's an English sheep dog.

Ex. 8
1. I am twelve and a half.
2. They are fourteen.
3. It is Andy's computer.
4. I am not thirteen.
5. That is not Kate's desk.
6. It is Mr Green's book.

Ex. 9
1. Where is it from?
2. His telephone number is 49675.
3. This panda is from China.
4. What's your telephone number?
5. That tiger is thirteen years old.

Ex. 10
1. Is it a comic?
2. What's this?
3. How old are you?
4. What's his telephone number?
5. Are you twelve?
6. Where is it from?

GRAMMAR CHECK

How old is *he/she/it*?
I *am*/We *are*/They *are*/He/*She*/*It is* twelve (years old).
Yes, I *am*. No, *I'm not*. Yes, it *is*. No, *it isn't*.
. . . *a* panda./ . . . *an* eagle.
Where is it *from*?
14 fourteen   15 fifteen   16 sixteen
17 seventeen   18 eighteen   19 nineteen
40 forty   50 fifty   60 sixty
70 seventy   80 eighty   90 ninety

LESSONS 1–10 Test your English

1. 1c 2a 3c 4c 5b 6b 7a 8c 9b 10c 11b 12a 13c 14b 15b
2. 1. my   2. is   3. a   4. His   5. He
   6. am   7. of   8. 's   9. She   10. Her
3. 1D   2H   3A   4J   5K   6C   7F
   8I   9B   10G

LESSONS 11–15

Ex. 1
1. Italy/Italian
2. Turkey/Turkish
3. Japan/Japanese
4. The USA/American
5. Greece/Greek
6. Spain/Spanish
7. Argentina/Argentinian
8. France/French   9. Britain/British

Ex. 2
1. She's from Spain. She's Spanish.
2. He's from the USA. He's American.
3. She's from Argentina. She's Argentinian.
4. She's from France. She's French.
5. He's from Greece. He's Greek.
6. He's from Brazil. He's Brazilian.
7. She's from Turkey. She's Turkish.
8. I'm from Italy. I'm Italian.

Ex. 3
1. Is Sylvia Greek?
2. Is Paul American?
3. Are Carlo and Laura Italian?
4. Is Mr Reuter German?
5. Is Mrs Domingo Brazilian?
6. Are Mr and Mrs Toyota Japanese?
7. Are you English?

Ex. 4
1. No, I'm not.
2. Yes, he is.
3. Yes, they are.
4. No, she isn't.
5. No, they aren't.
6. Yes, I am.
7. Yes, she is.
8. No, he isn't.

Ex. 5
1. Peter is not American.
2. Mr and Mrs Pellier are not French.
3. She is not Pat's teacher.
4. Miguel is not from Argentina.
5. Where is he from?
6. I am not Anne's brother.
7. Mary's eyes are not blue.

Ex. 6

1. Do you want a banana? No, thanks.
2. Do you want some chewing-gum? Yes, please.
3. Do you want some crisps? No, thanks.
4. Do you want an icream? Yes, please.
5. Do you want a sweet? Yes, please.
6. Do you want some chocolates? No, thanks.

Ex. 7

1. What colour are Linda's eyes? They're green.
2. What colour is John's hair? It's dark brown.
3. What colour is a tomato? It's red.
4. What colour are George's eyes? They're grey.
5. What colour is your hair? It's blonde.
6. What colour is the sky? It's blue.
7. What colour is Anne's hair? It's light brown.

Ex. 8

1. What nationality is he?
2. Are Mr and Mrs West from England?
3. Who's that man?
4. Do you want a chocolate?
5. Where's she from?
6. Is Maria Spanish?
7. What are your favourite colours?

GRAMMAR CHECK

Yes, you *are*/he *is*/ she *is*/it *is*/we *are*/you *are*/they *are*.

No, you *aren't*/he *isn't*/she *isn't*/it *isn't*/we *aren't*/you *aren't*/they *aren't*./
You're/He's/She's/It's/We're/You're/They're English.

LESSONS 16–20

Ex. 1

1. Whose sweater is this? It's Mike's.
2. Whose trainers are these? They're Kate's.
3. Whose watch is this? It's Mr Robson's.
4. Whose bike is this? It's Lucy's.
5. Whose boots are these? They're Linda's.
6. Whose camera is this? It's Miss Mason's.

Ex. 2

1. No, it isn't his.
2. Yes, they're hers.
3. Yes, it's mine.
4. No, it isn't hers.
5. No, they aren't his.
6. Yes, they're mine.
7. Yes, it's hers.
8. No, they aren't his.

Ex. 3

1. I don't like him. I think he's horrible.
2. Yes, I like them too. I think they're good.
3. I don't like it. I think it's bad.
4. I don't like her. I think she's boring.
5. I don't like them. I think they're horrible.
6. Yes, I like him too. I think he's great.
7. Yes, I like it too. I think it's fantastic.

Ex. 4

1. Has Miss Simpson got a cat?
2. Has David got any foreign stamps?
3. Have you got any rock star photos?
4. Has Mr Green got a bike?
5. Have you got any model trains?
6. Has Laura got a sleeping bag?

Ex. 5

1. No, I haven't.
2. Yes, she has.
3. No, he hasn't.
4. Yes, I have.
5. Yes, he has.
6. No, she hasn't.

Ex. 6

1. Peter's got some posters and some badges, but he hasn't got any stickers.
2. Liz's got some posters and some rock star photos, but she hasn't got any stickers.
3. George's got some stickers, but he hasn't got any badges or stamps.
4. Lucy's got some rock star photos, but she hasn't got any posters or stickers.
5. Mark's got some posters and some stamps, but he hasn't got any badges.
6. I've got some posters, but I haven't got any rock star photos or stamps.

Ex. 7

1. Mr Brown has got a computer.
2. What is this?
3. It is Andy's calculator.
4. She has got David's records.
5. He is Kate's father.
6. Who is that?
7. That is Miss Key's brother.
8. Peter has got a bike.

Ex. 8

1. Who's your favourite pop star?
2. Is this your jacket?
3. Are these Tom's jeans?
4. How many have you got?
5. Whose book is this?
6. Have you got a camera?

GRAMMAR CHECK

It's *yours/his/hers*.
I like *her/it/them*.
Have you *got* a brother?
Has he *got* a sister?
Has she *got* any sisters?

Yes, I *have*/he *has*/she *has*.
No, I *haven't*/he *hasn't*/she *hasn't*.

I've *got* a watch.
He's *got* a computer.
She's *got* some postcards.
I *haven't got* a watch.
He *hasn't got* a computer.
She *hasn't got* any postcards.

LESSONS 11–20

Test your English

1. 1b 2b 3a 4b 5a 6a 7b 8c 9b 10c 11c 12b 13c 14b 15c
2. 1. her 2. from 3. old 4. are 5. 's 6. him 7. they 8. 's 9. any 10. it
3. 1H 2D 3A 4I 5K 6C 7J 8E 9B 10G

LESSONS 21–25

Ex. 1

1. What's Mike's telephone number?
2. There's a poster in Lucy's room.
3. Where's Mr and Mrs Morgan's house?
4. Miss Green's got two cats.
5. It's her parents' house.
6. Is this Mary's jacket?
7. Yes, it's hers.
8. His name's Philip.

Ex. 2

1. What is Mike's telephone number?
2. There is a poster in Lucy's room.
3. Where is Mr and Mrs Morgan's house?
4. Miss Green has got two cats.
5. It is her parents' house.
6. Is this Mary's jacket?
7. Yes, it is hers.
8. His name is Philip.

Ex. 3

1. How many Turkish stamps are there? There are thirty.
2. How many German coins are there? There are thirteen.
3. How many Greek coins are there? There are eight.
4. How many Italian coins are there? There are twelve.
5. How many British records are there? There are sixty-eight.
6. How many American records are there? There are thirty-seven.

Ex. 4

1. Is there a desk? Yes, there is.
2. Is there a bathroom? No, there isn't.
3. Is there a bed? Yes, there is.
4. Are there any cupboards? Yes, there are.
5. Are there any pictures? No, there aren't.
6. Is there a carpet? Yes, there is.
7. Is there a chimney? No, there isn't.
8. Are there any curtains? No, there aren't.

Ex. 5

1. Where's the ball? It's on the box.
2. Where are the trainers? They're near the bed.
3. Where are the posters? They're on the door.
4. Where's the cupboard? It's next to the window.
5. Where are the cats? They're under the table.
6. Where's the carpet? It's on the floor.

Ex. 6

1. It's on the south coast of Wales.
2. It's in the east of England.
3. It's on the east coast of Scotland.
4. It's on the north-west coast of England.
5. It's on the south coast of England.
6. It's on the north-east coast of England.

Ex. 7

1. of 2. for 3. with 4. from 5. of 6. for 7. with

Ex. 8

1. Who 2. How many 3. Where 4. Whose 5. Where 6. How many 7. How

Ex. 9

1. Where's Mrs Thompson from?
2. How many foreign stamps has Anna got?
3. Where do you live?
4. How old is your father?
5. Whose book is this?
6. Who's that man?
7. How many students are there in your class?

GRAMMAR CHECK

Is there a chair/*Are* there any chairs in your room?
Yes, *there is/are.* No, *there isn't/aren't.*
There *is* a castle/*are* some gardens/*aren't any* parks in my town.
It's *in* the *north/south/east/west* of England.
It's *on* the *north/south/east/west* coast of Scotland.
I *live in* London. He *lives*/She *lives in* the centre *of* Liverpool.

LESSONS 26–30
Ex. 1
1. Do you want a comb or a brush?
   Can I have a brush, please?
2. Do you want a radio or a camera?
   Can I have a camera, please?
3. Do you want some jeans or some trainers?
   Can I have some jeans, please?
4. Do you want a football or a tennis racket?
   Can I have a tennis racket, please?
5. Do you want some badges or some stickers?
   Can I have some badges, please?

Ex. 2
1. Can Mrs Morgan play the piano? Yes, she can.
2. Can Paul use a computer? No, he can't.
3. Can you climb a rope? Yes, I can.
4. Can Kate and Andy dive? Yes, they can.
5. Can Mr Harrison speak Spanish? No, he can't.
6. Can your friends swim under water? No, they can't.

Ex. 3
1. George can dive but he can't swim under water.
2. Paul and Mary can use a calculator but they can't use a computer.
3. John can play tennis but he can't dive.
4. Miss Turner can play the guitar but she can't play the piano.
5. Mr West can ride a horse but he can't play tennis.

Ex. 4
1. writing   2. showing   3. knitting
4. playing   5. sitting   6. spelling
7. diving   8. dropping

Ex. 5
1. She's listening to the radio.
2. He's reading a comic.
3. She's talking on the phone.
4. They're watching TV.
5. He's writing a postcard.
6. I'm listening to a record.

Ex. 6
1. Is Diana listening to the radio? Yes, she is.
2. Is David reading a comic? Yes, he is.
3. Is your sister playing the guitar? No, she isn't.
4. Are your parents making an omelette? No, they aren't.
5. Is your little brother writing a postcard? Yes, he is.
6. Are you listening to a record? Yes, I am.

Ex. 7
1. She is wearing a jacket.
2. How do you spell your surname?
3. We can play the guitar very well.
4. Can I have a poster please?
5. Andy and Kate are running fast.
6. Is Mr Morgan making some toffee?

Ex. 8
1. Is he running in the marathon?
2. Do you want a record or a cassette?
3. How do you spell it?
4. Can you ride a horse?
5. Is she writing a letter?
6. What's your surname?

GRAMMAR CHECK

Can he dive/she knit/they ski?
Yes, he/she/we/they *can.*
No, he/she/we/they *can't.*

Are you *writing? Is* he *talking? Is* she *playing?*
Are we *listening? Are* they *running?*
Yes, I *am*/he is/she is/we *are*/they *are.*
No, I'm *not*/he isn't/she isn't/we aren't/they aren't.
You*'re diving.* He*'s playing.* She*'s speaking.*
We*'re swimming.* They*'re riding.*
You *aren't diving.* He *isn't playing.* She *isn't speaking.* We *aren't swimming.* They *aren't riding.*

LESSONS 21–30
Test your English
1. 1c 2b 3b 4c 5a 6b 7c 8b 9c
   10a 11c 12c 13b 14c 15b
2. 1. is 2. Its 3. there 4. of
   5. It 6. on 7. next 8. in
   9. any 10. an
3. 1E 2G 3B 4K 5D 6A 7J 8H 9I
   10C

LESSONS 31–35
Ex. 1
1. Mr Ward likes milk and orange juice, but he doesn't like coffee or tea.
2. Miss Grey likes fish and chips and apple pie, but she doesn't like hamburgers or chicken.
3. I like running and climbing, but I don't like swimming or windsurfing.
4. Liz likes coffee and tea, but she doesn't like milk or orange juice.
5. Alan likes swimming and climbing, but he doesn't like running or windsurfing.
6. Lucy likes hamburgers and fish and chips, but she doesn't like chicken or apple pie.

Ex. 2
1. Yes, I like them too. They're really nice.
2. Yes, I like it too. It's really nice.
3. Yes, I like them too. They're really nice.
4. Yes, I like it too. It's really nice.
5. Yes, I like them too. They're really nice.

Ex. 3
1. I don't. I like the blue ones.
2. I don't. I like the red one.
3. I don't. I like the green one.
4. I don't. I like the brown ones.
5. I don't. I like the pink one.

Ex. 4
1. these 2. that 3. these
4. Those 5. this 6. these 7. that

Ex. 5
1. Can you play tennis? Yes, I can.
   So can I.
2. Can you sail? No, I can't. Neither can I.
3. Can you windsurf? No, I can't. Neither can I.
4. Can you dive? Yes, I can. So can I.

Ex. 6
1. Yes, I do. So do I.
2. No, I don't. Neither do I.
3. No, I don't. Neither do I.
4. Yes, I do. So do I.
5. No, I don't. Neither do I.
6. Yes, I do. So do I.

Ex. 7
1. I like banana milkshakes.
2. Do you like hamburgers?
3. Sandra likes the blue sports bag.
4. He doesn't like visiting museums very much.
5. I like cheeseburgers with mustard.

Ex. 8
1. We've got Music on Tuesday afternoon.
2. No, we haven't.
3. Yes, we have.
4. When have you got History?
5. No, we haven't.
6. When have you got Library?
7. We've got French on Monday, Tuesday and Friday morning.
8. Yes, we have.

GRAMMAR CHECK

Do you like dancing? Yes, I *do.* No, I *don't.*
You *like* mustard. He *likes* milk. She *likes* chips.
You *don't like* onions. He *doesn't like* Coca-Cola.
She *doesn't like* ketchup.
Have we/you/they *got* Art on Monday?
Yes, *you/we/they have.* No, *you/we/they haven't.*
You*'ve*/They*'ve got* Maths on Tuesday.
We *haven't*/You *haven't*/They *haven't got* Music on Friday.

LESSONS 36–40
Ex. 1
1. How far is it from London to San Francisco? I don't know.
2. The radio's too loud. Turn it down please.
3. Peter's got about fifty American stamps. He hasn't got any French stamps.
4. Sheila's brother doesn't like German. He thinks it's too difficult.
5. We haven't got History on Thursday. We've got it on Friday.
6. Where's Mrs Hogwood from? I think she's Australian.

Ex. 2
1. 698 2. 1m 39cm 3. 345
4. 674km 5. 2,560mph 6. 786

Ex. 3
1. It's got small ears. It's black and white. It's got big spots. It lives in China. It's a panda.
2. It's got a long neck. It's very tall. It's got big spots. It lives in Africa. It's a giraffe.
3. It lives in South America. It's got a long tongue. It's got a long tail. It's an anteater.
4. It's grey. It's got soft fur. It lives in Australia. It's a koala bear.
5. It lives in Africa. It's got black and white stripes. It's a zebra.

Ex. 4
1. dangerous   2. short   3. long   4. high
5. long   6. expensive   7. heavy   8. short

Ex. 5
1. loudly   2. quiet   3. quietly   4. slow
5. fast   6. quickly   7. fast   8. slowly

Ex. 6
1. How many   2. Which   3. Where
4. Whose   5. What   6. How
7. When

Ex. 7
1. What's special about a zebra?
2. This programme isn't very interesting.
3. The Niagara Falls are 750 metres wide.
4. It's got a very long tongue.
5. Paul's homework is quite easy.
6. Which animal has got black and white stripes?

Ex. 8
1. When have we got History?
2. What's it like?
3. Do you want ketchup?
4. How tall are you?
5. Which shorts do you like?

GRAMMAR CHECK
... going *slowly* ... singing *quietly* ... smiling *nastily* ... running *fast*.
How tall are you? *I'm 1m 70cm tall.*
How high is Mount Everest?
It's 8,700 m high.
How long is the River Nile?
It's 4,132 miles long.
How far is it from Calais to Ostend?
It's 90 km.

LESSONS 31–40
Test your English
1. 1a 2b 3c 4a 5b 6a 7b 8a 9b 10c
   11b 12b 13b 14a 15c
2. 1. from   2. in   3. doesn't   4. of
   5. 've got   6. don't   7. On   8. but
   9. well   10. 'm
3. 1F 2G 3J 4A 5H 6K 7I 8B 9E 10C

LESSONS 41–45
Ex. 1
1. sausages   2. speeches   3. weeks
4. shells   5. dresses   6. witches
7. giraffes   8. branches   9. holidays
10. strawberries   11. toys   12. chimneys

Ex. 2
1. a   2. some   3. a   4. a   5. a
6. some   7. an

Ex. 3
1. any   2. some   3. any   4. some
5. any   6. some   7. any

Ex. 4
1. How much is a packet of biscuits? It's 29p.
2. How much is a Coke? It's 42p.
3. How much are the oranges? They're 15p each.
4. How much is a packet of crisps? It's 18p.
5. How much is a cup of tea? It's 35p.
6. How much are the apples? They're 12p each.
7. How much is an orange juice? It's 35p.
8. How much are the bananas? They're 30p each.

Ex. 5
1. It's half past three.   5. It's twenty to twelve.
2. It's quarter to six.   6. It's five past eight.
3. It's twenty past two.   7. It's twenty-five past ten.
4. It's ten to eight.   8. It's half past six.

Ex. 6
1. What time does the train leave?
   At twelve minutes past eight.
   What time does it arrive?
   At eighteen minutes past nine.
2. What time does the train leave?
   At sixteen minutes past nine.
   What time does it arrive?
   At twenty-seven minutes past ten.
3. What time does the train leave?
   At twenty-two minutes past ten.
   What time does it arrive?
   At twenty-nine minutes past eleven.

Ex. 7
1. Yes, it is.   2. It's cloudy./It's dull.
3. No, it isn't.
4. It's (warm and) sunny./It's hot./The sun is shining.
5. Yes, it is.
6. It's snowing./It's cold./It's freezing.

Ex. 8
1. What time does she go to bed?
2. What time do you have supper?
3. What time does he get up?
4. What time do they have breakfast?
5. What time do you have lunch?

Ex. 9
1. What do you do after breakfast?
   I go to school.
2. What do Bob and Alice do in the evening?
   They watch TV.
3. What does Mr Johnson have for breakfast?
   He has coffee and toast.
4. What does Sheila do after lunch?
   She does her homework.
5. What do you have for lunch?
   I have sandwiches.

Ex. 10
1. 'm writing.   2. plays   3. 's snowing
4. 's doing   5. has   6. watch

GRAMMAR CHECK
You *have* ... He *likes* ... She *likes* ...
It *rains* ... We *go* ... They *have* ...
What *do you do* ... *Does* he *like* ...
Does she *like* ... *Does* it *rain* ...
What time *do we have* lunch?
When *do they get up?*

LESSONS 46–50
Ex. 1
1. 17th   2. 1st   3. 12th   4. 20th
5. 30th   6. 11th   7. 16th   8. 22nd

Ex. 2
1. the first of January   2. the thirtieth of April
3. the twelfth of February
4. the twenty-fifth of December
5. the twenty-second of August
6. the eighteenth of March
7. the ninth of November   8. the third of May

Ex. 3
1. on   2. on   3. In   4. in   5. on
6. in   7. at   8. On

Ex. 4
1. No, he never plays video games.
2. Yes, I sometimes go swimming.
3. No, she never buys make-up.
4. Yes, I always make my bed.
5. Yes, he often buys magazines.
6. Yes, she usually does the washing-up.

Ex. 5
1. Does Peter like classical music?
   No, he doesn't.
2. Does Miss Bradford like house plants?
   Yes, she does.
3. Do you like chocolates? No, I don't.
4. Does Mr Redbury like ballet? Yes, he does.
5. Does Linda like jigsaws? No, she doesn't.
6. Does Tom like yogurt? No, he doesn't.
7. Does Mary like apples? Yes, she does.

Ex. 6
1. A: It's Mr Green's birthday on the thirty-first. What shall we get him?
   B: Let's get him some chocolates.
   A: No, let's get him a book.
2. A: It's Miss Bartlett's birthday on the third. What shall we get her?
   B: Let's get her some sweets.
   A: No, let's get her a sweater.
3. A: It's Peter's birthday on the eighteenth. What shall we get him?
   B: Let's get him some writing paper.
   A: No, let's get him some pens.

Ex. 7
1. When   2. which   3. What   4. What
5. When   6. Which   7. What

Ex. 8
1. Do you ever buy comics?
2. What's the date today?
3. Does Sandra like music?
4. What shall we get him?
5. What does 'bello' mean?
6. When's Pat's birthday?

GRAMMAR CHECK
What does 'Bienvenu!' mean? *It* means 'Welcome' in French.
How do you pronounce 'birthday'?
What's the date today? *It's* 11th February.
What date's/*When's* your birthday?
In September. *On* 2nd August.
Yes, he *does*. No, she *doesn't*.
What *shall* we buy David? *Let's* buy him a watch.

LESSONS 41–50 Test your English
1. 1c 2b 3a 4c 5a 6c 7b 8a 9b 10b
   11c 12b 13c 14a 15c
2. 1. on   2. at   3. For   4. or   5. In
   6. playing   7. to   8. It   9. like   10 does
3. 1H 2F 3K 4J 5A 6D 7I 8B 9C 10G

Look!				I am.			I'm not.	
Are	you they	watching TV?	Yes,	he she	is.	No,	he she	isn't.
Is	he she			we they	are.		we they	aren't.

6 Look at the pictures again. Write questions and answers using Yes (✓) or No (✗).

(Alan/write/a letter?)

Is Alan writing a letter?
Yes, he is.

(Alan/make/some toffee?)

Is Alan making some toffee?
No, he isn't.

1. (Diana/listen to/radio?)

Is Diana listen to radio?
Yes she is

2. (David/read/a comic?)

Is David read a comic?
No, he isn't

3. (your sister/play/the guitar?)

Is your sister playing the guitar?
Yes, she is

4. (your parents/make an omelette?)

Is your

5. (your little brother/write/postcard?)

Is your little brother write postcard? Yes, he is.

6. (you/listen to/record?)

Is your listen to record?

No, I don't

7 Write the words in the correct order.

can't / English / We / very well / speak

We can't speak English very well.

1. wearing / She / jacket / a / is

She is a wearing jacket

2. surname? / spell / you / How / do / your

How do you spell your su

3. play / can / the / very well / We / guitar

We can play guitar very well,

4. I / a / have / Can / please? / poster

Can I have poster please?

5. Andy / running / Kate / are / fast / and

Andy and Kate are fast reeming

6. Mr Morgan / toffee? / Is / some / making

Mr. mor. making some toffee?

31

8 **Write the questions in the correct places.**

Can you ride a horse?   What's she doing?
What's your surname?   Is she writing a letter?
How do you spell it?   Do you want a record or a cassette?
Is he running in the marathon?

What's she doing ? ....
She's doing her homework.

1. ....
   Yes, he is.

2. ....
   Can I have a cassette, please?

3. ....
   H – A – double R – I – S

4. ....
   Yes, I can but not very well.

5. ....
   No, she isn't.

6. ....
   Green.

Grammar check

Write the missing words.

Can

Interrogative

...Can.... you swim?
.... he dive?
.... she knit?
.... they ski?

Short answers

	I	...can.....		I can't.
	he	....		....
Yes,	she	....	No,	....
	we	....		....
	they	....		....

The present continuous

Interrogative

.Am..I   ....reading.?..........?(read)
.... you   ....?(write)
.... he   ....?(talk)
.... she   ....?(play)
.... we   ....?(listen)
.... they   ....?(run)

Short answers

	you	...are.....		you aren't.	
	I	....		I	
Yes,	he	....	No,	....	
	she	....		....	
	we	....		....	
	they	....		....	

Positive (short form)

I 'm studying......................   (study)
You ....   (dive)
He ....   (play)
She ....   (speak)
We ....   (swim)
They ....   (ride)

Negative (short form)

I'm not studying..........
....
....
....
....
....

Test your English

1 **Circle the correct answer.**

EMMA:	Can you swim, Paul?			
PAUL:	Yes, I can swim very	a) good	b) well	c) much
	Can you play the guitar?			
EMMA:	No, I can't, (1) .... I can play the piano.	a) and	b) or	c) but
PAUL:	Have you got a piano at home?			
EMMA:	Yes, I have. (2) .... in my room,	a) Its	b) It's	c) It's got
	(3) .... my desk.	a) next	b) near	c) on
PAUL:	Have you got a large house?			
EMMA:	No, (4) .... house is quite small.	a) ours	b) your	c) our
	(5) .... only one floor, with	a) There's	b) Their	c) Theirs
	a kitchen, a sitting room,			
	a bathroom and two bedrooms.			
	My (6) .... room is very big, but	a) parent's	b) parents'	c) parents's
	(7) .... is small.	a) my	b) me	c) mine
PAUL:	Is there a garden?			
EMMA:	Yes, (8)	a) there's	b) there is	c) there isn't
JOHN:	(9) .... do you live, Pete?	a) What	b) How	c) Where
PETE:	I live in Cardiff. That's (10)	a) on	b) in	c) next
	the south coast of Wales.			
JOHN:	Are there (11) .... interesting	a) some	b) an	c) any
	things to see in Cardiff?			
PETE:	Well, Cardiff is famous (12)	a) from	b) of	c) for
	its port, and there's also (13).........	a) any	b) an	c) a
	interesting museum.			
MOTHER:	Rita! Where are you?			
RITA:	I'm in my room. I (14) .... TV.	a) watching	b) 'm watch	c) 'm watching
MOTHER:	Do you want tea or coffee?			
RITA:	(15) .... I have tea, please?	a) Do	b) Can	c) Am

Total. ... 15

2 **Write the words in the correct places.**

It	Its	is	the	an	any	in	on	of	there	next

I live in Manchester, in ...*the*... north-west of England. Manchester (1) ....

a big, busy industrial city. It is also an important cultural centre. (2) ....

symphony orchestra is very famous and (3) .... is also a university.

My house is near the centre .... the city. (5) ....'s quite big.
There are two floors. My room is (6) .... the first floor, (7) ....
to my sister's room.

There are lots of things (8) .... my room. I've got lots of games, old toys,

models and photos. There aren't (9) .... pictures on the walls, but there's

(10) .... old poster above my bed.

Total ...../10

33

3 **Write the correct answers from the list on the right.**

JANE: Hello, Mark! How are you?

MARK: (F). I'm fine, thanks. ....

JANE: Are you doing your homework?

MARK: (1) ....

JANE: What are you doing?

MARK: (2) ....

JANE: Who's Marcel?

MARK: (3) ....

JANE: Where does he live?

MARK: (4) ....

JANE: How do you spell it?

MARK: (5) ....

JANE: Where's that?

MARK: (6) ....

        Can you speak French?

JANE: (7) ....

MARK: What languages are you learning at school?

JANE: (8) ....

MARK: Look, I've got some nice sweets and chocolates. Do you want a sweet or a chocolate?

JANE: (9) ....

MARK: Yes, here you are.

JANE: (10) ....

MARK: That's OK.

A. It's in the south of France.
B. He's my French penfriend.
C. Thanks very much.
D. N – I – C – E.
E. No, I'm not.
F. I'm fine, thanks.
G. I'm writing a letter to Marcel.
H. Only German.
I Can I have a sweet, please?
J. No, I can't.
K. He lives in Nice.

Total. . . . ./10

Grand Total. . ./35

Look!						
I You We They	like	coffee. playing tennis.	I You We They	don't	like	tea. swimming.
He She	likes		He She	doesn't		

1 Write what people like (✓) or don't like (✕).

		George	Nola	Mr Ward	Miss Grey	I	Liz	Alan	Lucy
FOOD	hamburgers	✓			✕				✓
	fish and chips	✕			✓				✓
	chicken	✓			✕				✕
	apple pie	✕			✓				✕
DRINKS	coffee			✕			✓		
	tea			✕			✓		
	milk			✓			✕		
	orange juice			✓			✕		
SPORTS	running		✕			✓		✕	
	swimming		✓			✕		✓	
	windsurfing		✓			✕		✕	
	climbing		✕			✓		✓	

George likes hamburgers and chicken but he doesn't like fish and chips or apple pie.
Nola likes swimming and windsurfing but she doesn't like running or climbing.

1. ....
2. ....
3. ....
4. ....
5. ....
6. ....

2 Agree with the statements.

I like the red sweater.

Yes, I like it too.

It's really nice.

I like the black roller skates.

Yes, I like them too.

They're really nice.

1. I like the white trainers.

   ....

   ....

2. I like the green sports bag.

   ....

   ....

3. I like the yellow shorts.

   ....

   ....

4. I like the brown track suit.

   ....

   ....

5. I like the black boots.

   ....

   ....

3 Disagree with the statements.

I like the yellow coat. (green)

I don't. I like the green one

I like the pink socks. (purple)

I don't. I like the purple ones

1. I like the orange trainers. (blue)

   ....

2. I like the black jacket. (red)

   ....

3. I like the white skirt. (green)

   ....

4. I like the blue shoes. (brown)

   ....

5. I like the silver anorak. (pink)

   ....

4 Write the correct word.

Do you want *this/these/those* badge?

this

1. Can I have *this/that/these* stamps, please?

   ....

2. I like *these/those/that* calculator.

   ....

3. Do you like *these/this/that* sports bags?

   ....

4. *These/Those/This* T-shirts over there are very nice.

   ....

5. She doesn't like *this/these/those* anorak.

   ....

6. Can I have *that/these/this* stickers, please?

   ....

7. Do you want *that/those/this* coat over there?

   ....

Look!					
Can you climb?	Yes,	I	can.	So	can I.
	No,		can't.	Neither	

Can	he she	play volleyball?	Yes, No,	he she	can. can't.

5 **Write short dialogues, using** Yes **or** No.

A: Can you play football ?

B: Yes, I can.

A: So can I.

A: Can you waterski ?

B: No, I can't.

A: Neither can I.

1.

A: Can you

B:

A:

2.

A: can you sail

B: Now, I can't

A: Neither can Y

3.

A: can you

B:

A:

4.

A:

B:

A:

37

Look!							
Do you like climbing?	Yes,	I	do.	So		do I.
	No,		don't.	Neither		

Does	he	like waterskiing?	Yes,	he	does.
	she		No,	she	doesn't.

6 Read the text, then complete the dialogue.

INDOOR SPORTS AND ACTIVITIES

Peter likes visiting museums and playing badminton, but he doesn't like painting or acting.

Rita likes playing badminton and working with computers, but she doesn't like doing gymnastics or dancing.

Roy likes working with computers and playing table tennis, but he doesn't like doing gymnastics or painting.

Diana likes playing table tennis and visiting museums, but she doesn't like dancing or acting.

RITA: Do you like playing badminton?

PETER: Yes, I do

RITA: So do I

ROY: Do you like doing gymnastics?

RITA: No, I don't

ROY: Neither do I

1. PETER: Do you like visiting museums?

   DIANA: Yes, I do

   PETER: No, I don't

2. RITA: Do you like dancing?

   DIANA: Yes, I do

   RITA: So do I

3. ROY: Do you like painting?

   PETER: No, I don't

   ROY: Neither do I

4. ROY: Do you like working with computers?

   RITA: Yes, I do

   ROY: So do I

5. PETER: Do you like acting?

   DIANA: Yes, I do

   PETER: No, I don't

6. DIANA: Do you like playing table tennis?

   ROY: Yes, I do

   DIANA: So do I

7 Write the words in the correct order.

doesn't / acting / She / very much / like

She doesn't like acting very much

1. like / milkshakes / I / banana

2. you / hamburgers? / like / Do

3. bag / Sandra / blue / sports / likes / the

4. museums / very much / He / like / visiting / doesn't

5. with / cheeseburgers / like / I / mustard

Look!						Monday.	
When have	we you they	got Art?	You We They	've got Art on		Tuesday	morning. afternoon.
Have	we you they	got Maths on Thursday?		Yes,	you	have.	
				No,	we they	haven't.	

8 Look at this timetable and write the questions or answers.

	MON	TUE	WED	THU	FRI
MORNING	Maths Drama English French	History French English Biology	Art Maths Geography History	English Maths Biology Art	Geography Maths French English
AFTER-NOON	Project Project	Music Library	Games Games	P.E. P.E.	

When have you got Drama?
We've got Drama on Monday morning.

4. ....
We've got History on Tuesday and Wednesday morning.

Have you got Games on Wednesday afternoon?
Yes, we have.

5. Have you got Geography on Thursday?
....

1. When have you got Music?
....

6. ....
We've got Library on Tuesday afternoon.

2. Have you got Biology on Friday morning?
....

7. When have you got French?
....

3. Have you got Project on Monday afternoon?
....

8. Have you got Maths on Monday morning?
....

Grammar check

Write the missing words.

Verb to like: **the present simple**

Interrogative

..............you like dancing?

Short answers

Yes, ..I do.....
No, ...

Positive

I	...like...	coffee.
You	....	mustard.
He	....	milk.
She	....	chips.

Negative (short form)

I	don't	tea.
You	....	onions.
He	....	Coca-Cola.
She	....	ketchup.

Verb to have (got): **plural**

Interrogative

.... we ..got..	
.... you	Art on Monday?
.... they	

Short answers

Yes,	....
	....
	....

No,	....
	....
	....

Positive (short form)

We	've got..	
You	....	Maths on Tuesday.
They	....	

Negative (short form)

We	....	
You	....	Music on Friday.
They	....	

1 Write these sentences, using capital letters, full stops, and apostrophes.

pauls got geography on tuesday morning its his best subject.

Paul's got Geography on Tuesday morning.

It's his best subject.

1. how far is it from london to san francisco? i dont know

How far is it from London to San Francisco? I don't know

2. the radios too loud turn it down please

The radio's too loud. Turn it down please.

3. peters got about fifty american stamps he hasnt got any french stamps

Peter's got about fifty American stamps. He hasnt got any French stamps.

4. sheilas brother doesnt like german he thinks its too difficult

Sheila's brother doesn't like German. He thinks it's to difficult.

5. we havent got history on thursday weve got it on friday

We haven't got history on Thursday. We've got it on Fraidy.

6. wheres mrs hogwood from? i think shes australian

Where's Mrs. Hogwood from? I think she's Australian.

2 Write the numbers in the boxes.

This bridge is one thousand two hundred and sixty-five metres long.

| 1,265 m |

1. There are six hundred and ninety-eight students in this school.

| 698 |

2. I am one metre thirty-nine centimetres tall.

| 1m 39cm |

3. She's got three hundred and forty-five stamps.

| 345 |

4. This river is six hundred and seventy-four kilometres long.

| 674km |

5. It flies at two thousand five hundred and sixty miles an hour.

| 2,560 mph |

6. There are seven hundred and eighty-six coins in this collection.

| 786 |

3 Write it, it's or it's got in the correct places. Then write the name of the animal.
Choose from:

zebra   panda   koala bear   elephant   anteater   giraffe

It...... lives in Africa. It's... grey. It's... very big. It's got big ears. It's... a(n) elephant.

1. It's got small ears. It's... black and white. It's got big spots. It... lives in China. It's a(n) ..... *panda*

2. It's got a long neck. It's... very tall. It's got big spots. It... lives in Africa.
It's... a(n) *giraffe*

3. It ...... lives in South America. It's got a long tongue. It's got a long tail.
It's a(n) *anteater*

4. It's... grey. It's got soft fur. It... lives in Australia.
It's... a(n) *koala bear*

5. It... lives in Africa. It's got black and white stripes. It's a(n) *zebra*.

4 Write the correct word.

I can't do this exercise. It's too *easy/difficult*.   difficult

1. He doesn't like climbing. He thinks it's too *dangerous/safe*.   dangerous

2. She's too *tall/short*. She can't reach that book.   short

3. She doesn't like school. She thinks her school days are too *short/long*.   long

4. He can't climb down the tree. It's too *low/high*.   high

5. I can't spell this word. It's too *long/short*.   long

6. I like these trainers, but they're too *cheap/expensive* for me.   expensive

7. Can you help me? This box is too *heavy/light* for me.   fast

8. He likes going on holiday. He thinks his school holidays are too *long/short*. short

42

Look!				
Adjectives	quick	nice	nasty	fast
Adverbs	quickly	nicely	nastily	fast

5 **Write the adjective or the adverb in the correct place.**

(loud) Turn down the TV! It's too ..loud...........

(quick) She's speaking very ....quickly.....

1. (loud)   I can't hear you. Speak more ..loudly....
2. (quiet) You're too noisy! Be ...quiet......!
3. (quiet) She's singing too ...quietly.....
4. (slow)   I don't like this car. It's too ...slow.....
5. (fast)   You're swimming too ...fast......!
6. (quick) Can you say this word ...quickly....?
7. (fast)   That's a very ...fast..... boat.
8. (slow)   They are walking very ...slowly...

6 **Write** What, Which, Who, Whose, When, Where, How, **or** How many **in the spaces.**

......Who......'s that woman?

That's Madonna.

1. ...How may..badges have you got?

About thirty.

2. ...Which...... sports bag do you like?

The green one.

3. ...Where...... do you live?

In New York City.

4. ...Whose.... shoes are these?

They're Lucy's.

5. ...What...... 's the matter?

My homework's too difficult!

6. ...How......... long is the Mississippi?

I don't know!

7. ...When...... have we got Biology?

On Tuesday and Friday morning.

7 Write the words in the correct order.

animal / has / long / This / neck / a

This animal has a long neck.

1. about / What's / zebra? / special / a

....

2. isn't / programme / interesting / This / very

....

3. 750 / The / wide / are / metres / Niagara Falls

....

4. a / 's got / very / It / tongue / long

....

5. is / Paul's / easy / quite / homework

....

6. and / black / Which / got / white / animal / stripes? / has

....

8 Write the questions in the correct places.

How tall are you?   Do you want ketchup?
What's it like?   Which shorts do you like?
When have we got History?   How far is it?

How far is it?..
It's 314 kilometres.

1. ....
   On Monday morning.

2. ....
   It's black, and it's got soft fur.

3. ....
   No, thanks.

4. ....
   I'm 1 metre 65 centimetres tall.

5. ....
   Those.

Grammar check

Write the missing words.

I'm quick. I'm walking	quickly.
You're slow. You're going	....
She's quiet. She's singing	....
He's nasty. He's smiling	....
It's fast. It's running	....

....	are you?	.... 1 m 70 cm ....
....	is Mount Everest?	.... 8,700 m ....
....	is the River Nile?	.... 4,132 miles ....
....	is it from Calais to Ostend?	.... 90 km.

1 **Circle the correct answer.**

MIKE:	What are your best subjects?			
RUTH:	My best subjects are History and Geography.			
	What are ....?	a) you	(b)) yours	c) your
RUTH:	I (1) .... Games and PE.	a) like	b) doesn't like	c) likes
MIKE:	(2)	a) I do so.	b) So I do.	c) So do I.
RUTH:	(3) .... have you got PE?	a) What	b) Where	c) When
MIKE:	(4) .... Monday and Wednesday.	a) On	b) At	c) In
	What about you?			
RUTH:	(5) .... it on Tuesday and	a) We got	b) We've got	c) Have we got
	Friday.			
RUTH:	What sports do you like?			
MIKE:	Well, my favourite sports are football			
	and swimming. I (6).......... diving, and I	a) don't like	b) likes	c) doesn't like
	can't water ski.			
RUTH:	(7)	a) I can neither.	b) Neither can I.	c) Neither I can.

PAUL:	Look! (8) .... roller skates	a) Which	b) What	c) How
	do you like?			
EMMA:	I like (9)	a) this	b) these	c) that
PAUL:	The blue ones? I (10) .... I like the black	a) do	b) like	c) don't
	ones and (11) .... pink anorak over there.	a) those	b) that	c) these
EMMA:	Yes, I (12) .... it too.	a) do	b) like	c) don't

PETE:	Look at this picture. It's the Brooklyn Bridge			
	in New York City.			
JOHN:	How (13) ....?	a) is it long	b) long is it	c) it is long
PETE:	It's 486 metres long.			
JOHN:	Wait a moment! I (14) .... hear you! The	a) can't	b) do	c) can
	radio's (15) .... loud. Turn it off!	a) not very	b) quite	c) too

Total. ... /15

2 **Write the words in the correct places.**

m	have	don't	doesn't	On	of	in	from	old	well	but

Hello! My name's Bruno Martini. I'm twelve years ...old... I'm Italian.

I come (1) .... Rome, but I live (2) .... Milan now.

I have a sister and a brother. My sister lives with me, but my brother (3) ....

live at home. He lives and works in Naples, in the south (4) .... Italy.

I go to school in the city centre. I'm in Class 1B. We (5) .... five lessons

every day except Sunday. My favourite subject is Art. I (6) .... like Maths

– I hate it! It's too difficult for me.

(7) .... Tuesday and Thursday afternoon I have swimming classes. I'm a good

swimmer, (8) .... I can't dive very (9) .... At school I (10) ....

Total. ... /10

also learning how to use a computer.

3 Write the correct answers from the list on the right.

In a fast food restaurant.

SYLVIA: What do you want, Sophia?

SOPHIA: (D) Can I have a milkshake, please? ....

SYLVIA: Which flavour do you want?

SOPHIA: (1) ....

SYLVIA: Do you want a cake with it?

SOPHIA: (2) ....

SYLVIA: OK. Two banana milkshakes, please.

MAN: Here you are.

SYLVIA: (3) ....

SOPHIA: I have some French homework to do.

SYLVIA: When have you got French?

SOPHIA: (4) ....

SYLVIA: I don't like French.

SOPHIA: (5) ....

It's not very easy. I'm learning German too.

SYLVIA: Really? I have German lessons in the evenings.

SOPHIA: Do you like German?

SYLVIA: (6) ....

But I can't speak it very well.

SOPHIA: (7) ....

What's your school like?

SYLVIA: (8) ....

SOPHIA: How far is it from your home?

SYLVIA: (9) ....

SOPHIA: Anyway, I must go. It's late! See you!

SYLVIA: (10) ....

A. On Tuesday and Friday morning.
B. It's new and quite big.
C. Yes. Bye!
D. Can I have a milkshake, please?
E. It's about four kilometres.
F. Banana, please.
G. No, thanks.
H. Neither do I.
I. Neither can I.
J. Thank you.
K. Yes, I do.

Total. ... 10

Grand Total. ... /35

Look!	*Singular*		*Plural*
most words	orange, tiger, sister	+ *s*	oranges, tigers, sisters
words ending in -*y*	city, country, baby	+ *ies*	cities, countries, babies
words ending in -*ay*, -*ey*, -*oy*	day, journey, boy	+ *s*	days, journeys, boys
words ending in -*s*, -*sh*, -*ch*, -*x*	bus, brush, peach, box	+ *es*	buses, brushes, peaches, boxes
Irregular plurals	man, woman, child, foot		men, women, children, feet

1 **Write the plurals of the words.**

nut .... *nuts* ....   3. week ....   8. branch ....

inch ...... *inches* ...   4. shell ....   9. holiday ....

activity . *activities* ....   5. dress ....   10. strawberry ....

1. sausage ....   6. witch ....   11. toy   ....

2. speech ....   7. giraffe ....   12. chimney ....

2 **Write a, an, or some in the spaces.**

There's ... *a* ..... school near here.

I'd like . *some* . apples, please.

1. I'd like .... packets of nuts, please.

2. There are .... peaches on the table.

3. Do you want .... chocolate?

4. I'd like .... cup of coffee, please

5. Can I have .... Coke, please?

6. I've got .... crisps.

7. That's .... apple pie.

3 **Write some or any in the spaces.**

I'd like .. *some* ... oranges, please.

Have you got ... *any* .... biscuits?

1. Liz hasn't got .... badges.

2. I'd like .... peaches, please.

3. Is there .... milk?

4. There are .... students over there.

5. Are there .... interesting things to see here?

6. I'd like .... cheese and biscuits.

7. Has he got .... foreign stamps?

4 **Write questions and answers.**

MENU

apples......12p each   cup of tea......35p

oranges....15p each   cup of coffee...40p

peaches....23p each   Coke............42p

bananas....30p each   orange juice....35p

packet of biscuits...29p

packet of crisps......18p

(cup of coffee?)   How much is a cup of coffee?
It's 40p.

(peaches?)   How much are the peaches?
They're 23p each.

1. (packet of biscuits?)

2. (Coke?)

3. (oranges?)

4. (packet of crisps?)

5. (cup of tea?)

6. (apples?)

7. (orange juice?)

8. (bananas?)

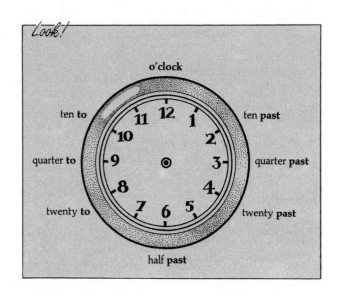

Look!

o'clock

ten to   ten past

quarter to   quarter past

twenty to   twenty past

half past

6 Write questions and answers.

London To Birmingham	
Dep.	Arr.
7.14	8.23
8.12	9.18
9.16	10.27
10.22	11.29

5 Write the times.

What time is it?

10.00   It's ten o'clock.

1.15   It's quarter past one.

1. 3.30   ....

2. 5.45   ....

3. 2.20   ....

4. 7.50   ....

5. 11.40   ....

6. 8.05   ....

7. 10.25   ....

8. 6.30   ....

What time does the train leave? ....

At fourteen minutes past seven. ....

What time does it arrive? ....

At twenty-three minutes past eight. ....

1. ....
....
....
....

2. ....
....
....
....

3. ....
....
....
....

7 Answer the questions about the weather.

What's the weather like?

It's raining.

3. Is it hot?

Is it snowing?

No, it isn't.

4. What's the weather like?

1. Is the sun shining?

5. Is it wet?

2. What's the weather like?

6. What's the weather like?

Look!

What time	do	I we you they	go to school?	You I We They	go	to school at 8.30.
	does	he she		He She	goes	

8 Write the questions.

What time do you have breakfast ? .... I have breakfast at seven o'clock.

1. .... She goes to bed at half past ten.

2. .... We have supper at quarter to eight.

3. .... He gets up at half past seven.

4. .... They have breakfast at eight o'clock.

5. .... I have lunch at half past one.

9 **Write questions and answers.**

(Mary/do in the afternoon?) What does Mary do in the afternoon?

(play/with her friends) She plays with her friends.

1. (you/do after breakfast?) ....

    (go/to school) ....

2. (Bob and Alice/do in the evening?) ....

    (watch/TV) ....

3. (Mr Johnson/have for breakfast?) ....

    (have/coffee and toast) ....

4. (Sheila/do after lunch?) ....

    (do/her homework) ....

5. (you/have for lunch?) ....

    (have/sandwiches) ....

10 **Write the correct verb form.**

(go) Diana usually ..goes... to bed at ten o'clock.

(rain) What's the weather like? It's raining.............. again!

1. (write) What are you doing? I .... a letter.

2. (play) She sometimes .... tennis at school.

3. (snow) Hey, look! It ....!

4. (do) Be quiet! Bob .... his homework.

5. (have) My sister usually .... lunch at one o'clock.

6. (watch) I usually .... TV in the evening.

Grammar check

Write the missing words.

The present simple

Positive

(go)	I ..... _go_	to bed at nine o'clock.
(have)	You.	lunch at one o'clock.
(like)	He	coffee.
(like)	She	coffee too.
(rain)	It	a lot here.
(go)	We	riding after lunch.
(have)	They	eggs for breakfast.

Interrogative

(I/live)	Where .do I live.?	
(you/do)	What	in the evening?
(he/like)	....	tea?
(she/like)	....	fish?
(it/rain)	....	much here?
(we/have)	What time	lunch?
(they/get up)	When ....?	

1 **Write the numbers in the boxes.**

My birthday is on the twenty-first of June.

| 21st |

I think it's on the third of October.

| 3rd |

1. Sue's birthday is on the seventeenth of March.

| |

2. Its' on the first of June!

| |

3. Leslie's birthday – on the twelfth!

| |

4. He's arriving on the twentieth.

| |

5. Their birthday is on the thirtieth of September.

| |

6. I think it's on the eleventh.

| |

7. Not the sixteenth!

| |

8. Remember the meeting on the twenty-second of July!

| |

2 **Write the dates.**

13/10   the thirteenth of October........

6/7   the sixth of July...................

1. 1/1 ....

2. 30/4 ....

3. 12/2 ....

4. 25/12 ....

5. 22/8 ....

6. 18/3 ....

7. 9/11 ....

8. 3/5 ....

Look!

PREPOSITIONS In ... on ... at

In

Months
in March/August

Seasons
in the spring/the summer

Parts of the day
in the morning/the afternoon

On

Days
on Sunday/Monday morning

Dates
on 2nd June/15th November

At

Times
at three o'clock/half past four

3 **Write in, on or at in the spaces.**

I get up ..... *at* ..... six o'clock.

Her birthday is .... *in* ...... September.

1. Kate's birthday is .... 22nd July.

2. We've got Biology .... Thursday.

3. .... which month is your birthday?

4. They usually do their homework .... the afternoon.

5. Do you go to school .... Saturday morning?

6. My birthday is .... the summer.

7. School starts .... 8.30.

8. .... which day of the week have you got Science?

Look!				
I			my	
You	always		your	
We	usually	tidy	our	
	often			room.
They	sometimes		their	
He	never		his	
		tidies		
She			her	

4 **Write the answers.**

Do you ever go swimming?

(Yes/often) Yes, I often go swimming.

Does she ever play tennis?

(No/never) No, she never plays tennis.

1. Does Paul ever play video games?

   (No/never) ....

2. Do you ever go swimming?

   (Yes/sometimes) ....

3. Does Miss Newell ever buy make-up?

   (No/never) ....

4. Do you ever make your bed?

   (Yes/always) ....

5. Does Mr Portlock ever buy magazines?

   (Yes/often) ....

6. Does Brenda ever do the washing-up?

   (Yes/usually) ....

Look!	I you we they	like video games?	Yes,	I we they	do.	No,	I we they	don't.
Do								
Does	he she			he she	does.		he she	doesn't.

5 Write questions and answers, using Yes (✓) or No (✕).

(you/fish soup?)   ✓   Do you like fish soup? Yes, I do. ....

(Sheila/computer games?)   ✕   Does Sheila like computer games? No, she doesn't..

1. (Peter/classical music?)   ✕   ....

2. (Miss Bradford/house plants?)   ✓   ....

3. (you/chocolates?)   ✕   ....

4. (Mr Redbury/ballet?)   ✓   ....

5. (Linda/jigsaws?)   ✕   ....

6. (Tom/yogurt?)   ✕   ....

7. (Mary/apples?)   ✓   ....

6 Write short dialogues.

(Maria's birthday / 12th / mug / sweets)

A: It's Maria's birthday on the twelfth.
What shall we get her?...................

B: Let's get her a mug.....................

A: No, let's get her some sweets. ....

1. (Mr Green's birthday / 31st / chocolates / book)

   A: ....

   ....

   B: ....

   A: ....

2. (Miss Bartlett's birthday / 3rd / sweets / sweater)

   A: ....

   ....

   B: ....

   A: ....

3. (Peter's birthday / 18th / writing paper / pens)

   A: ....

   ....

   B: ....

   A: ....

7 Write what, when or which in the spaces.

.**What**. day is it today?

1. .... 's your birthday?

2. In .... season is Roy's birthday?

3. .... 's 'yes' in Japanese?

4. .... 's the weather like?

5. .... does she go to bed?

6. .... pen do you want, the blue one

   or the red one?

7. .... time is dinner?

8 Write the questions in the correct places.

What does 'bello' mean?   Does Sandra like music?
When's Pat's birthday?   How do you pronounce 'tights'?
Do you ever buy comics?   What shall we get him?
What's the date today?

How do you pronounce 'tights' ?
TIGHTS.

1. ....
   No, never.

2. ....
   It's 15th July.

3. ....
   Yes, she does.

4. ....
   Let's get him a radio.

5. ....
   It means 'beautiful' in Italian.

6. ....
   It's on 2nd December.

Grammar check

Write the words in the correct places.

What   What's   What does   When   How   does   doesn't
Let's   shall   It   It's   On   In

| .... 'Bienvenu!' mean? | .... means 'Welcome!' in French. |

| .... do you pronounce 'birthday'? |

| .... the date today? | .... 11th February. |

| .... date | .... September. |
| .... 's your birthday? | .... 2nd August. |

| Does | he / she | like dogs? | Yes, | he | .... |
| | | | No, | she | .... |

| What .... we buy David? | .... buy him a watch. |

56

1 Circle the correct answer.

At the station

PETE:	What time is it?			
JOHN:	It's .... eight.	a) half to	b) half past	c) half
	What time (1) ....?	a) the train leaves	b) leaves the train	c) does the train leave
PETE:	(2) .... ten to nine.	a) In	b) At	c) On
JOHN:	I'm hungry. I (3) .... something to eat.	a) 'd like	b) don't like	c) like
	Look, there's a coffee bar over there.			

At the coffee bar

JOHN:	(4) .... are the peaches?	a) How many	b) How	c) How much
PETE:	They're 23p (5)	a) each	b) pence	c) altogether
JOHN:	Mm .... no, I'd like a packet of biscuits.			
	Excuse me, have you got (6) .... biscuits?	a) some	b) a	c) any
WOMAN:	Yes, (7)	a) I've	b) I have	c) I've got
JOHN:	(8) .... I have a packet, please?	a) Can	b) Do	c) Am
WOMAN:	Yes, here you are. That's 40p.			
JOHN:	Thank you.			

PETE;	When's Susan's birthday?			
JOHN:	It's (9) .... 3rd July.	a) in	b) on	c) at
PETE:	Let's (10) .... her a present.	a) getting	b) get	c) gets
JOHN:	Yes, but what sort of present? (11) .... books?	a) She does like	b) Likes she	c) Does she like
PETE:	No, she doesn't like (12) .... very much. She (13) .... buys books or magazines.	a) read	b) reading	c) reads
		a) always	b) often	c) never
JOHN:	But she likes music.			
	(14) .... we get her a record?	a) Shall	b) Do	c) Are
PETE:	Yes, that's a good idea. Hurry up, now.			
	The train (15) ....!	a) leaves	b) leaving	c) 's leaving

Total ....../15

2 Write these words in the correct places.

| It | does | 'm | like | playing | In | For | to | at | on | or |

Dear Anna,

How are you? I'm fine. I'm happy because I ....'m.... finishing

school for the summer soon, (1) .... 12th June.

Let me tell you something about my typical day. I get up (2) ...at...... quarter past seven, have a shower and get dressed. (3) ....on breakfast I have toast and marmalade and a cup of tea (4) ...or... coffee. Then I go to school.

(5) ....In.... the afternoon I usually do my homework, but I also like (6) .playing. football with my friends. After supper we often watch TV. I go (7) ...to.... bed quite early.

Here in Rome the weather is nice. (8) ....'s warm and sunny.

What's the weather (9) ....in England now?
        Write soon.
        Best wishes,
        Paolo

P.S. What (10) .... 'snake' mean?

Total ...../10

3 **Write the correct answers from the list on the right.**

Alan and Diana are at a holiday camp.

ALAN: The weather's horrible today.

DIANA: (E) Yes, it's really dull

ALAN: What time is lunch?

DIANA: (1) It is a quarter to one

ALAN: Well, I'm thirsty. What shall we have?

DIANA: (2) ....

ALAN: OK. Two Cokes and a packet of nuts, please.

MAN: (3) ....

ALAN: Thank you. How much is it altogether?

MAN: (4) .... (J.) ....

DIANA: Do you help in the house, Alan?

ALAN: (5) ....

DIANA: What do you do?

ALAN: (6) ....

DIANA: Do you ever do the washing up?

ALAN: (7) ....

DIANA: Lucky you! I do lots of things at home.

ALAN: Do you get pocket money?

DIANA: (8) ....

ALAN: By the way, when's your birthday?

DIANA: (9) ....

ALAN: Mine is in the summer too. What time is it now?

DIANA: (10) ....

ALAN: Is it? Time for lunch! Hurry up!

A. Yes, I do.
B. Yes, I usually spend it on clothes.
C. It's in August.
D. Well, I make my bed and tidy my room.
E. Yes, it's really dull.
F. Let's have a Coke.
G. It's twenty to one.
H. It's at quarter to one.
I. No, never.
J. That's £1.20, please.
K. Here you are.

Total ....../10

Grand Total ...../35

59

Longman Group UK Limited,
Longman House, Burnt Mill, Harlow,
Essex CM20 2JE, England
and Associated Companies throughout the world.

© Longman Group UK Limited 1988
First published 1988
Fifth impression 1992

Set in 11/12^1/$_2$ pt Palatino

Produced by Longman Singapore Publishers Pte Ltd.
Printed in Singapore

ISBN 0 582 018234